COULD YOU EVER
DIVE WITH DOLPHINS!?

Written by
Sandra Markle

Illustrated by
Vanessa Morales

Scholastic Inc.

For Jim Smalley
and all the children at
J.W. Reason Elementary
School in Hilliard, Ohio.

Acknowledgments: The author would like to thank the following people for sharing their enthusiasm and expertise: Gretchen Lovewell, Program Manager for Mote Marine Laboratory Stranding Investigations Program and Dr. Randall Wells, Director of the Chicago Zoological Society's Sarasota Dolphin Research Program in Sarasota, Florida. A special thank-you to Skip Jeffery for his loving support during the creative process.

Photos ©: back cover center left: Jeff Rottma/Alamy Stock Photo; back cover center right: Jeff Rottma/Alamy Stock Photo; back cover bottom left, 1: Andrea Izzotti/Shutterstock; 4: zorazhuang/Getty Images; 6: Animal Stock/Alamy Stock Photo; 8: Humberto Ramirez/Getty Images; 10: Doug Perrine/Alamy Stock Photo; 12: Jeff Rottma/Alamy Stock Photo; 14: Blue Planet Archive/Alamy Stock Photo; 16: John Russell/Alamy Stock Photo; 18: Losrodri/Getty Images; 20: Jeff Rottma/Alamy Stock Photo; 22: by wildestanimal/Getty Images; 24: Karen Debler/Alamy Stock Photo; 26: Jeff Rottma/Alamy Stock Photo; 30–31: xingmin07/Getty Images; 32: Losrodri/Getty Images.

Library of Congress Cataloging-in-Publication Data available

ISBN 978-1-338-85876-1

10 9 8 7 6 5 4 3 2 1   23 24 25 26 27

Printed in China   38
First edition, June 2023

Book design by Maria Lilja

What if one day when you woke up, you weren't quite yourself? What if your whole world had changed? What if you were in the ocean living with BOTTLENOSE DOLPHINS!?

Bottlenose dolphins swim fast, ride currents, and surf big waves. Sometimes, dolphins leap out of the water to look around for fish to eat. Or, possibly, just for fun!

4

When you live with dolphins, you will surf like a champion without needing lessons.

FACT

Bottlenose dolphins can leap as high as 20 feet out of the water.

Bottlenose dolphins breathe air. So, when they dive, they hold their breath. When they surface, dolphins breathe in through their blowholes.

A blowhole is the opening on top of a dolphin's head. As dolphins dive, the muscles around the blowhole relax and snap it shut.

When you live with dolphins, you will easily hold your breath long enough to explore sunken treasures.

FACT

Bottlenose dolphins can hold their breath for up to 13 minutes.

Bottlenose dolphins are very social. They live in groups the way people live in neighborhoods. These groups change with ages and life stages. Nursery groups are mothers with calves. Juvenile groups are youngsters hanging out together.

Pairs of adult males may spend their lives together, helping each other find food and stay safe while they're seeking to become fathers.

When you live with dolphins, you will always be part of a group.

FACT

In places with lots of seafood, bottlenose dolphins form super groups of 1,000 or more individuals.

Bottlenose dolphins are predators that mainly dine on squid and fish. Sometimes, when they find a lot of fish in shallow water, they'll have a dinner party.

First, the dolphins flip their tail fins, called flukes. That stirs up the ocean bottom and creates a wall of dirty water, trapping fish. Then, they tail-swat fish to each other. GULP! GULP!

When you live with dolphins, you will eat seafood for breakfast, lunch, and dinner. Snacks, too!

FACT

Bottlenose dolphins only ever have one set of teeth—80 to 100 total. Each is cone-shaped and sharp-tipped.

Flying fish are speedy seafood, and bottlenose dolphins use a trick to catch them. While a flying fish is airborne, this predator swims upside down just below the surface. Then, the dolphin snags the flying fish when it plops back into the ocean.

When you live with dolphins, you will sometimes eat fast food, but you'll need to be clever to catch a mouthful!

FACT

Bottlenose dolphins' eyes let them see nearly all the way around themselves. So, they don't miss spying seafood or danger.

Bottlenose dolphins don't open their mouths to make sounds. Instead, they inhale and push air back and forth between their lungs and air sacs in their heads. That's how dolphins make whistles, grunts, trills, squeaks, and squawks.

As a calf, a dolphin makes a unique whistle. That becomes its signature whistle—its name. And other dolphins make that whistle to get its attention.

SQUEAK, SQUAWK!

When you live with dolphins, you will create your own whistle name. And you'll grunt, trill, squeak, and squawk with friends.

FACT

Bottlenose dolphin whistles can be heard underwater from a mile away.

What is a dolphin's favorite game?
Salmon says!

While learning to hunt, dolphin calves watch and mimic adults. One trick some youngsters learn is to chase a fish into a giant, empty shell. Next, the dolphin pokes its nose into the shell, swims to the surface, and pushes the shell out of the water. PRESTO! The fish drops into the dolphin's mouth.

When you live with dolphins, you will be on an all-you-can-catch diet.

FACT

Bottlenose dolphins swallow fish headfirst so any spiny fins fold flat and won't stick in their throats.

Echolocation (ek-oh-loh-**kay**-shuhn) is what a dolphin uses to sense its ocean world. First, it blasts out clicks—as many as 1,000 per second. The echoes of those sounds are picked up as vibrations by the dolphin's jawbone. These travel to its ears, which send signals to its brain. Then, the dolphin senses the shape, size, and thickness of whatever bounced back the echoes.

When you live with dolphins, you will play tag even in dark ocean places and never bump into anything.

FACT

Using echolocation, bottlenose dolphins sense things as small as a golf ball from 200 feet away.

Playing allows bottlenose dolphin calves to practice twisting and turning while swimming. Playing also lets youngsters in a group learn to work together. Someday, what dolphin calves learn by playing will be used as adult survival skills.

When you live with dolphins, you will play catch with anything you pick up—even turtles, fish, and octopuses, if they let you.

FACT

Bottlenose dolphins flip fish out of the water with their tail flukes. This stuns the fish, making them easy-to-catch seafood.

Bottlenose dolphins are predators, but they are also prey to other ocean hunters, such as sharks. So, when dolphins sense an enemy, they swim fast to flee. Then, just as they practiced, they twist and turn to be harder to chase.

FACT

Bottlenose dolphins swim as fast as 20 miles per hour.

23

If bottlenose dolphins don't have time to escape, they find safety in numbers. Since calves are much smaller than adults, they are most at risk. So, adults quickly surround youngsters. And any dolphin a shark comes close to slaps this enemy hard with its fins.

When you live with dolphins, your group will make any shark that comes close scram—FAST!

FACT

Bottlenose dolphins also use their thick, strong snouts to ram any attacker.

A bottlenose dolphin swims while it sleeps. It can do that because half of its brain rests while the other half stays awake. After about two hours, its brain switches which side is on duty. So, while resting, a dolphin still surfaces as needed to breathe and keeps alert for danger. To stay safe, a calf always naps close to its mother.

When you live with dolphins, you will never have bedtime. You can sleep and still check out cool ocean creatures.

FACT

Bottlenose dolphins close just one eye at a time while sleeping.

Luckily, you don't have to choose. You will always be who you are and live where people live.

WHERE DO BOTTLENOSE DOLPHINS LIVE?

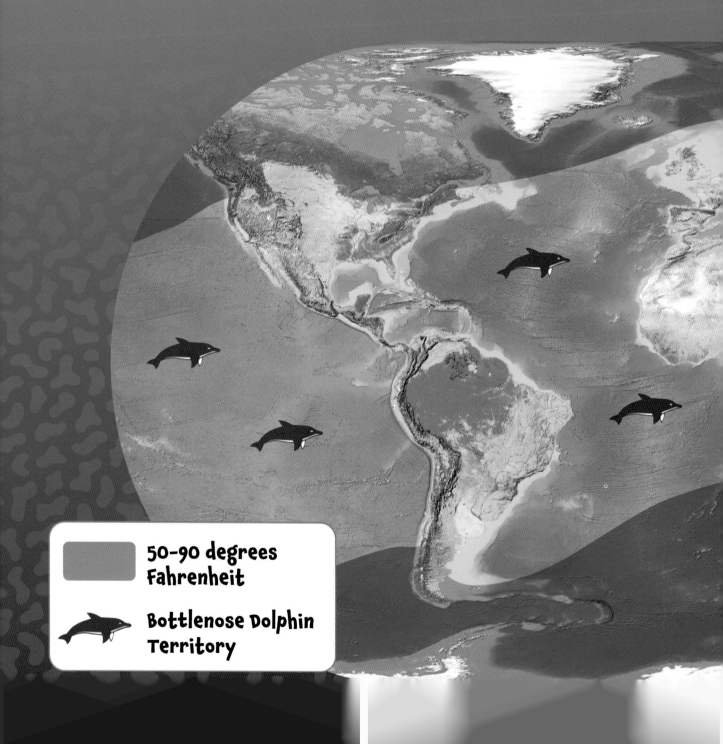

	50-90 degrees Fahrenheit
	Bottlenose Dolphin Territory

Bottlenose dolphins live in oceans all around the world except the Arctic and Antarctic Oceans. They mainly live in shallow water close to shore. Some, however, live in deep water far from shore. But bottlenose dolphins live only where waters are comfortably warm.

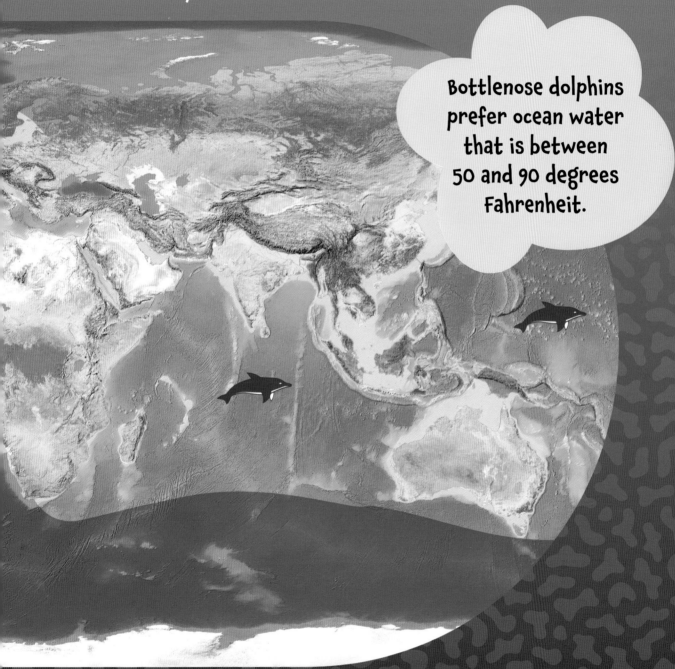

Bottlenose dolphins prefer ocean water that is between 50 and 90 degrees Fahrenheit.

FUN FACTS!

At birth, a bottlenose dolphin calf is around 4 feet long and weighs as much as 40 pounds. How does that compare to how big you were when you were born?

A bottlenose dolphin calf develops its signature whistle when it is as young as a month old.

Bottlenose dolphins completely shed their outermost layer of skin about every two hours. That way their bodies stay smooth to slip easily through the water.

Bottlenose dolphins do something similar to a cough by blasting air out their blowholes.